ANTIQUE DOLLHOUSE

Coloring

Enchanting Miniature Worlds to Color & Explore

YUMIKO TEZUKA

Small rooms
of nuts

Life of the rabbits.

Coloring Techniques

Before you get started coloring, I've included some of my favorite tips and tricks to help you achieve beautiful results. Colored pencils work well for these illustrations, but feel free to use whatever art supplies you like best—you can even use different coloring mediums within the same illustration!

Lecturer: Yumiko Tezuka

❈ HOW TO COLOR FLOWERS

1. Apply a light layer of reddish purple to the petals to create a base.

2. Add yellow to the tips of some of the petals.

3. When coloring the leaves, add yellow green to the tips. Using two different shades of green will create a more complex look.

❈ HOW TO COLOR LIGHT

1. Color the wall, leaving the area where the light hits white.

2. Color the edges of the area left white in step 1 with yellow and orange. The goal is to create a blurry outline around the light.

3. Add more yellow and orange to create a gradated effect, but leave the center white.

❧ HOW TO COLOR PASTRIES

1. Use light orange to create a base for the cookies, muffins, breads, and other baked goods.

2. Use darker colors for the fillings and paper liners.

3. Apply a layer of ocher or brown on top to give the baked goods a delicious golden brown look.

❧ HOW TO COLOR A SCENE

1. Color the inside of the nut and the flowers. For a cohesive look, use similar colors for all the flowers.

2. Color the bear and accessories. Use similar colors for the scarf, rug, and decor.

3. Add more color to shaded areas to create a three-dimensional effect.

❧ HOW TO COLOR PEOPLE

1. Color the skin pale orange and apply a light layer of ocher to color the hair.

2. When coloring the clothes, make some areas darker to create subtle shading.

3. Add a bit of color to the cheeks. Use your favorite color for the eyes.

How to Create the Antique Look

To create a muted, antique look, limit the overall number of colors used within the illustration. The key is to opt for subdued colors rather than bright ones. If using colored pencil, layer brown, yellow, or gray on top of bright colors to create an antique finish. You can also add light brown or cream to white areas to add subtle shading.

Tips & Tricks

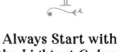

1

Always Start with the Lightest Colors

To create a three-dimensional effect, apply light colors first and check the overall balance before applying darker layers.

2

Create Subtle Shading

Instead of filling an area with a single color, apply 2-3 shades of the same color or leave some areas white. This will create a three-dimensional effect.

3

Test Out Your Color Scheme

If you're having trouble deciding which colors to use, make a photocopy of the illustration to test out the colors you're considering.

Introduction

Did you have a dollhouse when you were a child? Do you remember how each room looked and all the pretty little furniture inside? Did your dollhouse have lights that actually turned on or music that played out loud? Every dollhouse offers the opportunity to escape reality and step into a magical world. For this reason, dollhouses are beloved not only by children, but by adults around the world.

Dollhouses were first built in 16th century Europe and served as a way for wealthy adults to display and store expensive miniature objects. By the 19th century, dollhouses became a popular plaything for middle and upper class girls. One of the most famous dollhouses in history was built in the 1920s for Queen Mary, wife of King George V of England. Queen Mary's dollhouses included contributions from the finest artists and craftsmen of the time and even had electricity and running water! This dollhouse was made in 1:12 scale, where one foot in real life is reduced to one inch in the dollhouse. This has since become the international standard for most dollhouses. Scale is important when it comes to dollhouses; otherwise, furniture and other miniatures can look "off."

This coloring book contains 27 scenes from three large dollhouses and seven smaller houses and shops. My hope is that coloring these decorated dollhouses and miniatures makes you feel as if you are an inhabitant of one of these enchanting abodes!

—Yumiko Tezuka

The Classic House

Nine rooms for dolls.

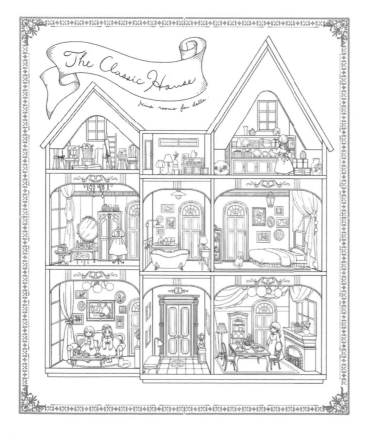

🌸 The Classic House
Nine Rooms for Dolls

This house was inspired by the architecture of fine European cities. If you look closely, you will see that each room is filled with special details and unique residents. Enjoy coloring the woodwork, flooring, and furnishings in this elegant home.

The Dressing Room

The Dressing Room

❀ *The Classic House*
The Dressing Room

Imagine getting ready every morning in your very own dressing room, full of pretty dresses, chic accessories, and elegant shoes. There's even a vanity table with all sorts of lotions, potions, and perfumes!

The Drawing Room

The Drawing Room

🌸 *The Classic House*
The Drawing Room

The drawing room is the perfect location for afternoon tea. There's a cozy settee for sitting and a gallery wall full of pretty paintings.

The Bedroom

Start Date:

Finish Date:
_____

Notes:

The Bedroom

❀ *The Classic House*
The Bedroom

Imagine sleeping in this stately bedroom, complete with a large comfy bed, elegant draperies, and gallery wall of pretty paintings.

The Dining Room

The Dining Room

The Classic House
The Dining Room

Dinner is served! This cozy dining room contains a wood-burning fireplace, china cabinet, and unique chandelier. The table is set for two.

Kitchen

🌸 *The Classic House*
Kitchen

It's time for breakfast in this cute little kitchen. On today's menu: pancakes. When coloring the girl's hair, consider the way the strands are arranged in the braid to create a three-dimensional effect.

Collection Room

Start Date:

Finish Date:

Notes:

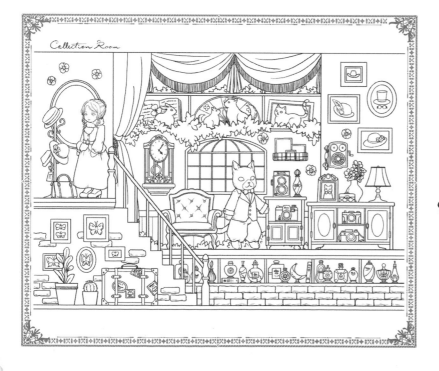

Collection Room

🌸 The Classic House
Collection Room

Imagine an entire room designed for displaying treasures collected over the years. Look closely and you'll find perfume bottles, a camera, paintings, and all sorts of interesting specimens. Each and every one has its own unique story, just like the residents of the house.

Miniature Goods

Miniature Goods

❀ *The Classic House*
Miniature Goods

Wearing hats and parasols, the residents of this house
enjoy picnics by the creek on weekends. Draw your favorite
pattern on a dress or hat to create your own original textile.

Miniature House

❀ *The Classic House*
Room in the Lantern

Dollhouses inspire limitless creativity—there can be entire worlds located inside an unassuming object. In this scene, the interior of a lantern is transformed into a cozy room full of twinkling lights. Check out the coloring technique guide at the beginning of the book for tips on coloring lights.

Inside the teapot

Inside
the
teapot

🌸 *Miniature House*
Inside the Teapot

This room inside a teapot features cute teapot-shaped lights and a spout door. Keeping the curve in mind, color the surface of the teapot as evenly as possible to create a smooth texture.

Small
rooms
of nuts

Small rooms of nuts

✿ Miniature House
Small Rooms of Nuts

Talk about miniature, these rooms are located inside nuts!
Each room depicts its resident enjoying one of the four seasons.

The Country House

Life in the Countryside

🌸 *The Country House*
Life in the Countryside

This house was designed for relaxing and enjoying nature. There is space to read, write, and rest. If you decide on a color theme for your house first, it will be easier for you to select colors for the smaller items.

Miniature Cottage

🌸 *The Country House*
Miniature Cottage

This picturesque cottage is set among a forest of trees and flowers. There's even a small well. The exterior of the house features classic stone walls and a thatched roof.

Miniature Foods

Start Date:

Finish Date:

_____

Notes:

Miniature Foods

🌸 *The Country House*
Miniature Foods

Fresh herbs from the garden are used abundantly in the dishes
on the dining table. When you color food, imagine the delicious
texture and smell of fluffy baked bread, warm and hearty stew, and
so on to help make your art more realistic.

Countryside Garden

🌸 *The Country House*
Countryside Garden

There is a small garden located in front of the window, which the residents take very good care of. If the overall color scheme starts to feel monotonous with all the green and brown, try incorporating colorful hues for the window frames, flower pots, and other objects to provide sharp contrast.

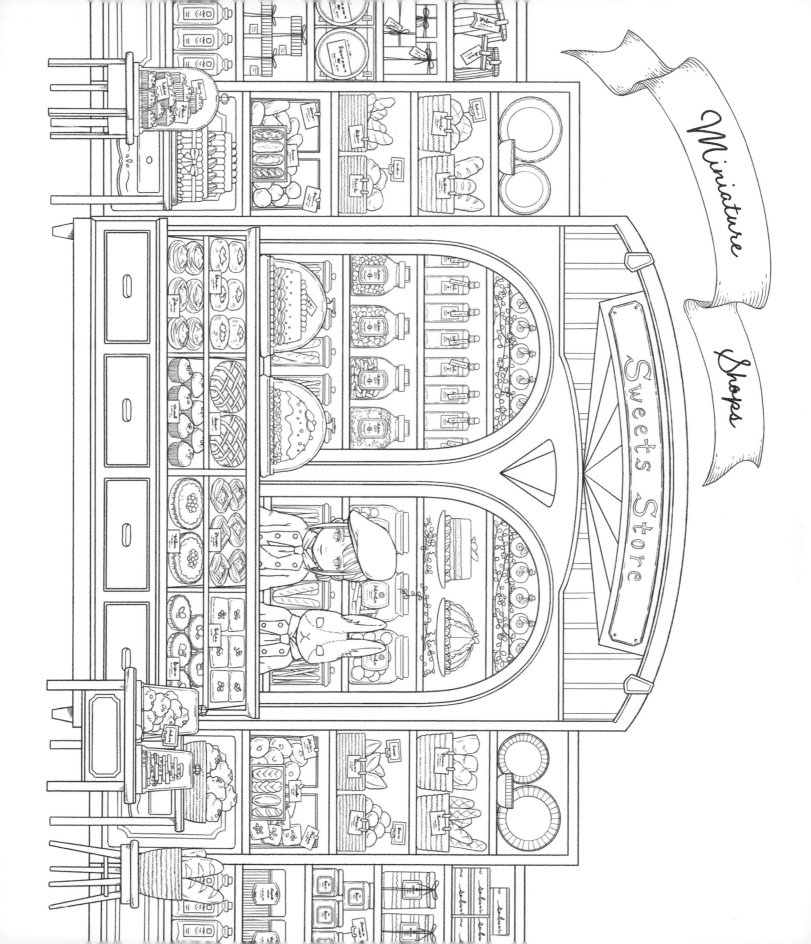

Start Date:

Finish Date:

_____

Notes:

🌸 *Miniature Shops*
Sweets Store

Now, let me introduce a village of miniature shops and their owners. This is a very popular sweets shop in town. The walls are lined with pastries and other baked goods.

❀ *Miniature Shops*
Bookstore

This small bookstore has been located in the heart of town for a long time. Both the building and the sign are in the shape of a book. The inside of the shop is small, but it has been designed well so that customers can easily see the books, and there are many old books neatly lined up on the second floor.

Start Date:

Finish Date:
_____

Notes:

🌸 Miniature Shops
Flower Shop

This flower shop is located on the edge of a beautiful field. It offers a wide selection of seasonal cut flowers that grow in the field, as well as potted plants. In fact, the shop is always lined with lots of flowers. The arrangements made by the rabbit florist who owns the shop are quite popular.

🌸 *Miniature Shops*
Knick Knack Shop

The walls of this knick knack shop are lined with a variety of goods collected by the owner. To color neatly, begin by applying a light color to the walls and shelves first, and then color the small items on display. Think about the order in which the items are layered from the back to the front as you color.

Life of the rabbits.

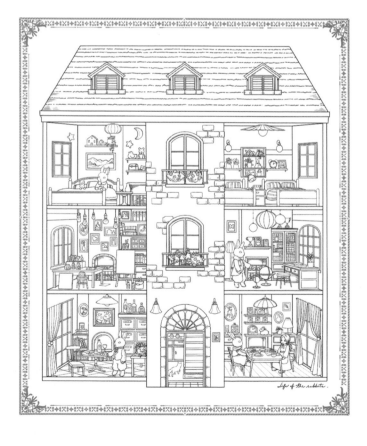

🌸 *The House of Rabbits*
Life of the Rabbits

This three-story house is inhabited by a family of rabbits. If you look closely, you'll see that all the figurines and paintings are rabbit motifs! Use slightly different colors to give each rabbit its own unique personality and tell a story.

The Art Studio

Start Date:

Finish Date:
_____

Notes:

The Art Studio

❀ *The House of Rabbits*
The Art Studio

This room is a blank canvas just waiting to be colored. An easel, brushes, and paint are all set up, ready for the artist in residence to get to work when inspiration strikes.

The Library

Start Date:

Finish Date:

Notes:

The Library

🌸 *The House of Rabbits*
The Library

Shelves full of books and drawers full of files line the walls of this cozy library complete with a roaring fire. It's the perfect place to curl up with a good book on a cold evening.

The Study

The Study

🌸 *The House of Rabbits*
The Study

This cozy room is ideal for sitting by the fire and reading a book or planning your next big adventure. Trophies, mementos, and other curiosities are displayed throughout the space.

The Dining Room

Start Date:

Finish Date:

_____

Notes:

The Dining Room

🌸 *The House of Rabbits*
The Dining Room

This picturesque dining room is a wonderful setting
for a meal to be shared between friends.

The House of Rabbits

✿ The House of Rabbits
Miniature Goods

For this page, color the illustrations and then cut out along the light gray lines. Next, fold along the dotted lines to create three-dimensional figures that can be arranged in the rooms on the next couple of pages.

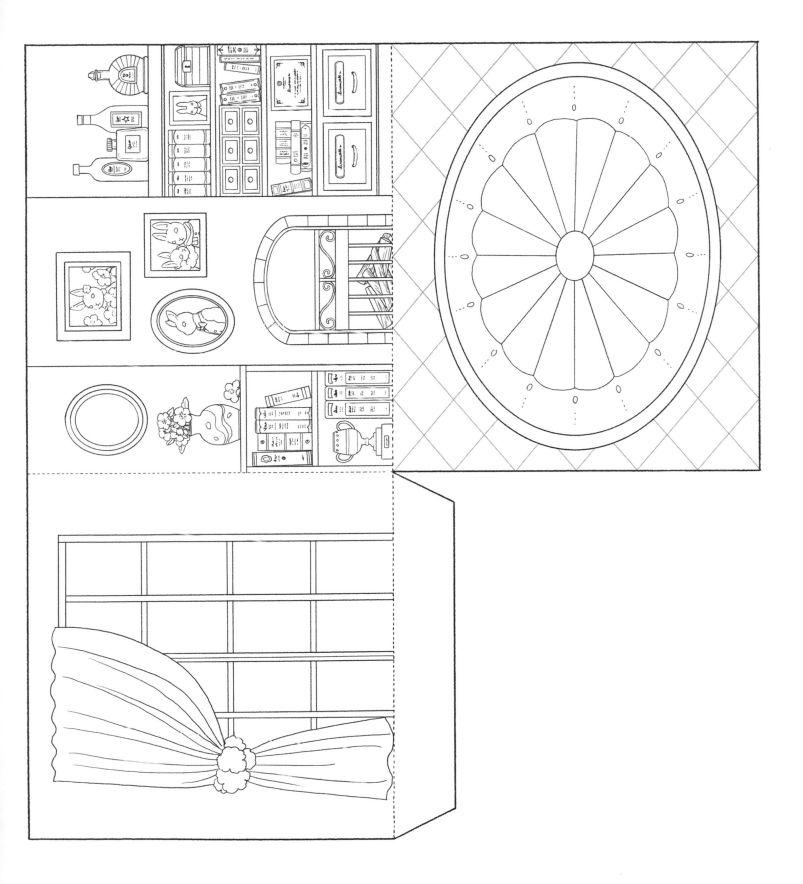

Start Date:

Finish Date:

_____

Notes:

🌸 *The House of Rabbits*

After coloring this page, cut out along the outline of the illustration. Fold all the dotted lines into valley folds and glue the margins to the back side of the floor section to create a three-dimensional room. Have fun arranging the dolls and accessories you made on the previous page.

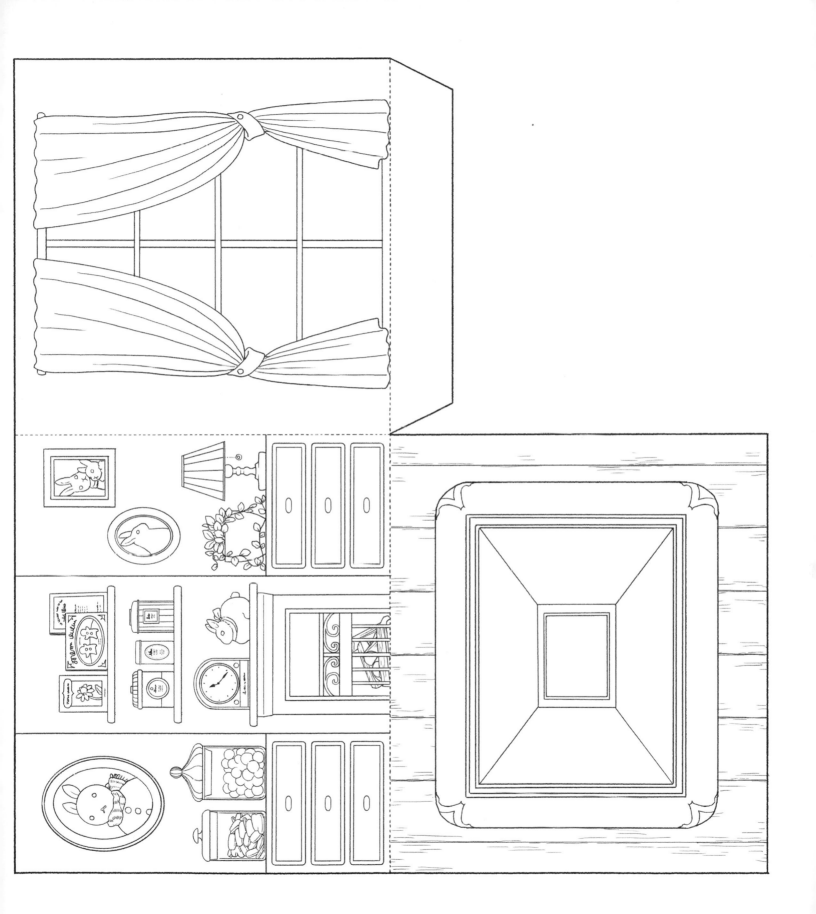

Start Date:

Finish Date:

Notes:

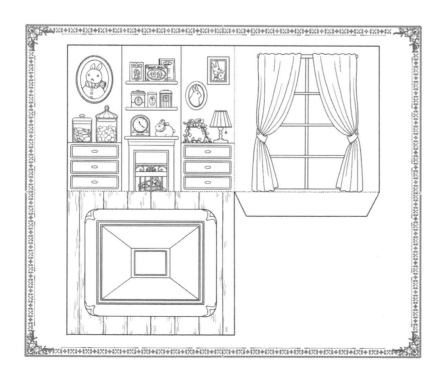

❀ *The House of Rabbits*

After coloring this page, cut out along the outline of
the illustration. Fold all the dotted lines into valley
folds and glue the margins to the back side of the
floor section to create a three-dimensional room.
Have fun arranging the dolls and accessories you
made a few pages prior.

About the Author

Yumiko Tezuka is a freelance illustrator known for her storybook-style artwork featuring dolls, animals, and other vintage-inspired goods. She is the author of multiple coloring books in Japan and has also created illustrations for jigsaw puzzles and paper goods. Visit her website at yumikt.com and follow her on Instagram @yumiko_tezuka.

Antique Dollhouse Coloring
First Published in 2024 by Zakka Workshop, a division of World Book Media LLC

www.zakkaworkshop.com
134 Federal Street
Salem MA 01970 USA
info@zakkaworkshop.com

OTONA JOSHI NO ZEITAKU JIKAN DOLLHOUSE NURIE
All rights reserved. Copyright ©Yumiko Tezuka 2021

Original Japanese edition published by Oizumi Co., Ltd. English language rights, translation & production by World Book Media LLC arranged through The English Agency (Japan) Ltd.

Issuer: Shinya Suzuki
Illustration: Yumiko Tezuka
Design: Power Design Co., Ltd.
Translator: Namiji Singley
English editor: Lindsay Fair

ISBN: 978-1-940552-82-8

Printed in China
10 9 8 7 6 5 4 3 2 1